Created and Written
by
Larry Wolfe Horwitz

HALLMARK PRESS INC.

HALLMARK PRESS INC.
New York • Miami

Library of Congress Catalog Card Number: 89-81742

ISBN 0-9624895-0-6

Printed in the United State of America

For information address Hallmark Press Inc, New York Office:
207 West 25th Street, 7th Floor, New York, New York 10001

First Edition
1 2 3 4 5 6 7 8 9 10

Dedicated:

TO WOMEN

IN THE BATTLE OF THE SEXES
There are times when women are victorious.
There are times when men are victorious.
Sometimes there is a draw.

In this book I'm handing the women of the
world that final victory.

Use it, abuse it,* cherish it—

BECAUSE IT'S YOURS!

*WARNING SERIOUS INJURY MAY RESULT IF CAPTIONS DEPICTED
ARE USED ON A LIVE HUSBAND.

Special thanks to Solomon Roskin, Nancy Kaplan, Kevin Powel, Larry Eisenberg, Phil McLeod and the many others for their creative and inspirational support without which this book would not have been possible.

CONTENTS

HOW TO USE A DEAD HUSBAND FOR...

CHAPTER
ONE

HOW TO USE A DEAD
HUSBAND FOR...
BEAUTIFYING YOUR HOME

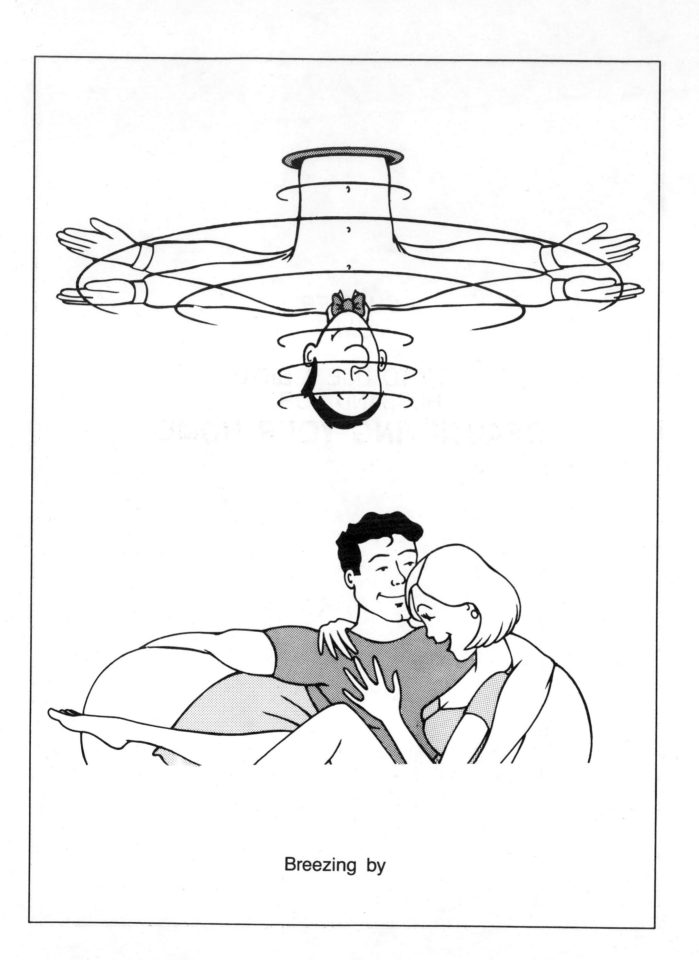

Breezing by

The fountain!

The door mat

Toilet roll holder

The Thinker

"DEAD HUSBAND"

POP art for the dining room

Perfect memory

Litter box

A clean bird is a health bird

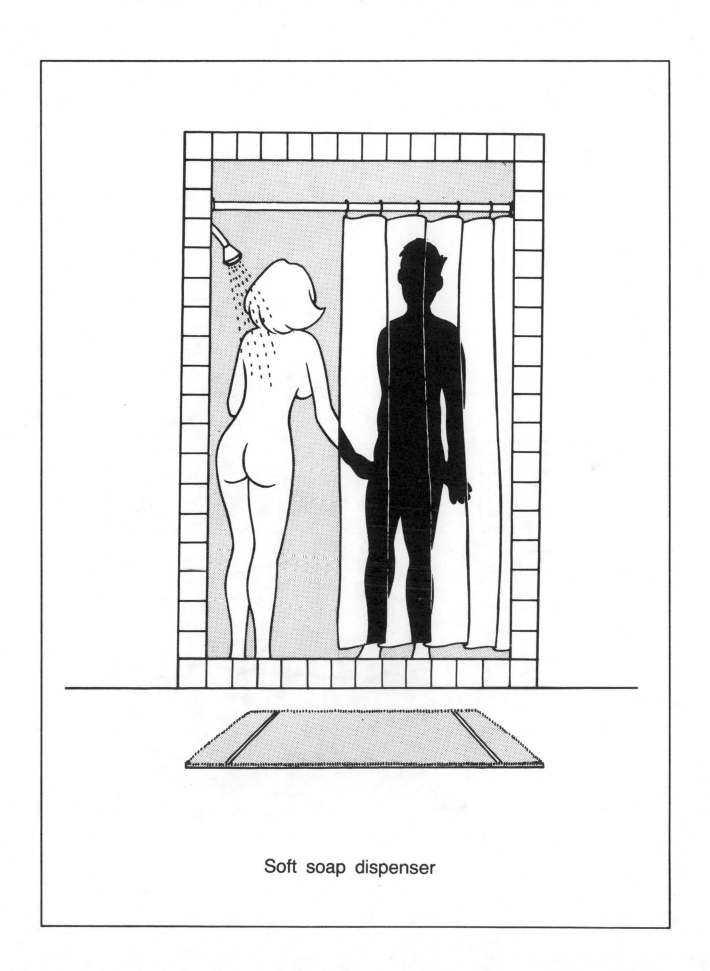

Soft soap dispenser

Garbage disposal unit

The family tree

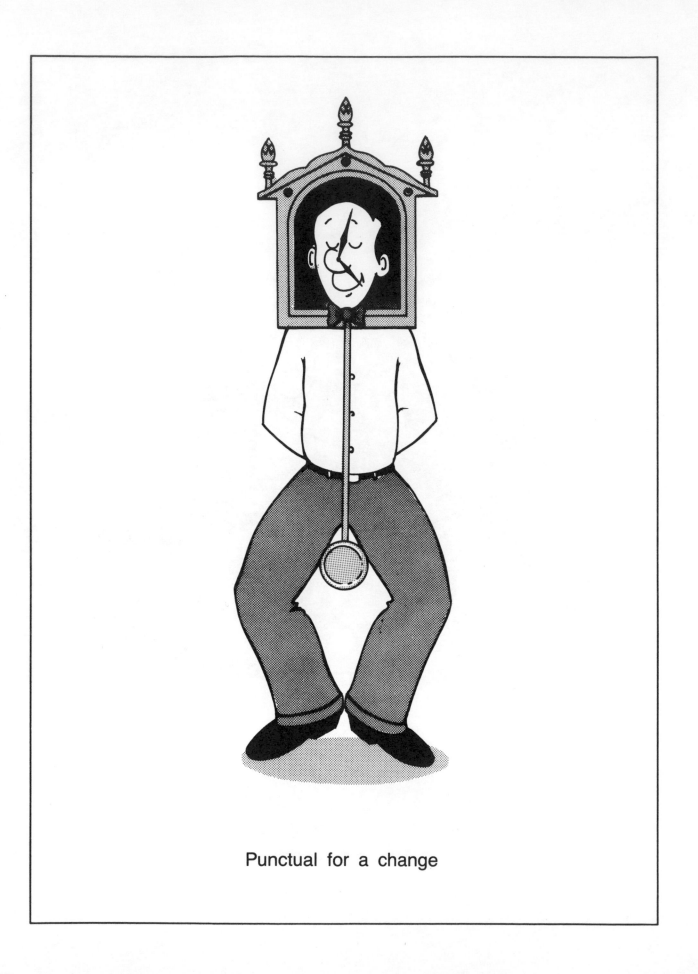

Punctual for a change

Towel rod

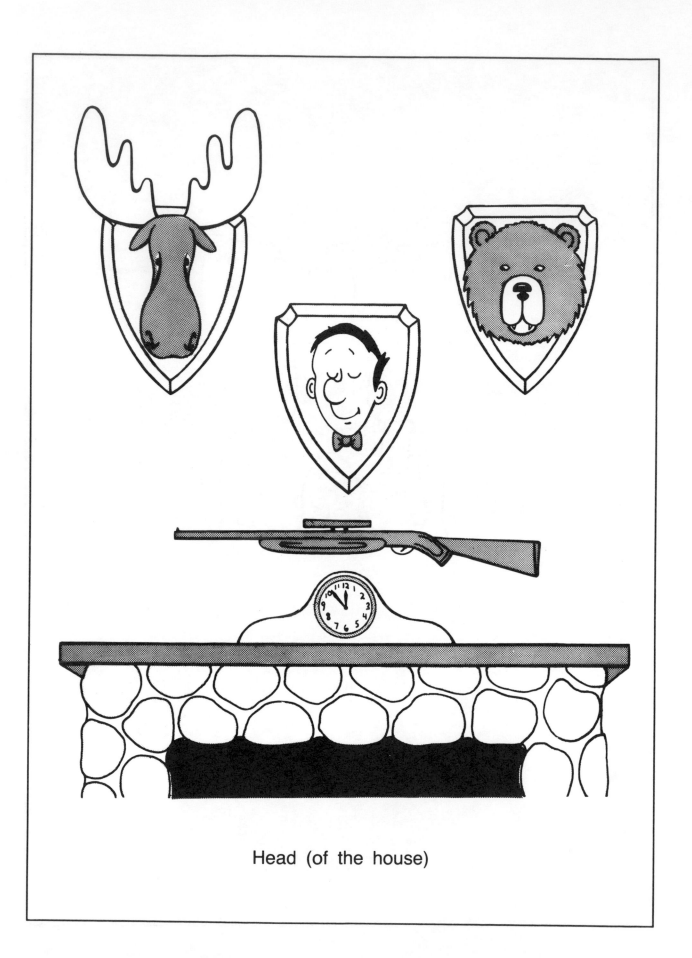

Head (of the house)

You light up my life

*CHAPTER
TWO*

HOW TO USE A DEAD
HUSBAND FOR...
ENTERTAINING

The morning after

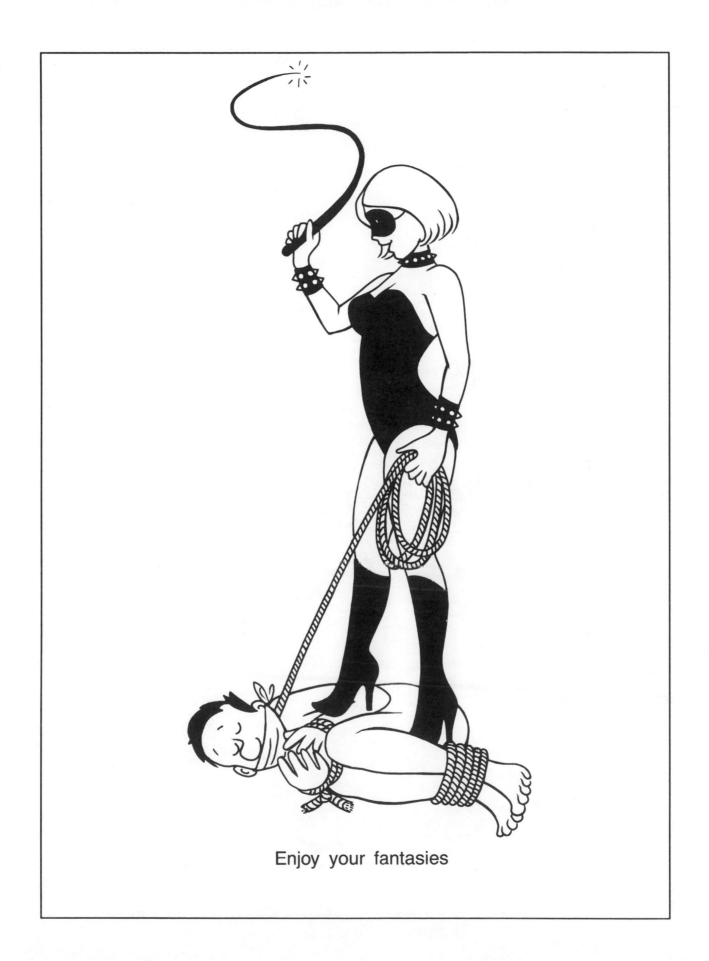

Enjoy your fantasies

Ice bucket

Thanksgiving day dinner

Thanksgiving Day parade

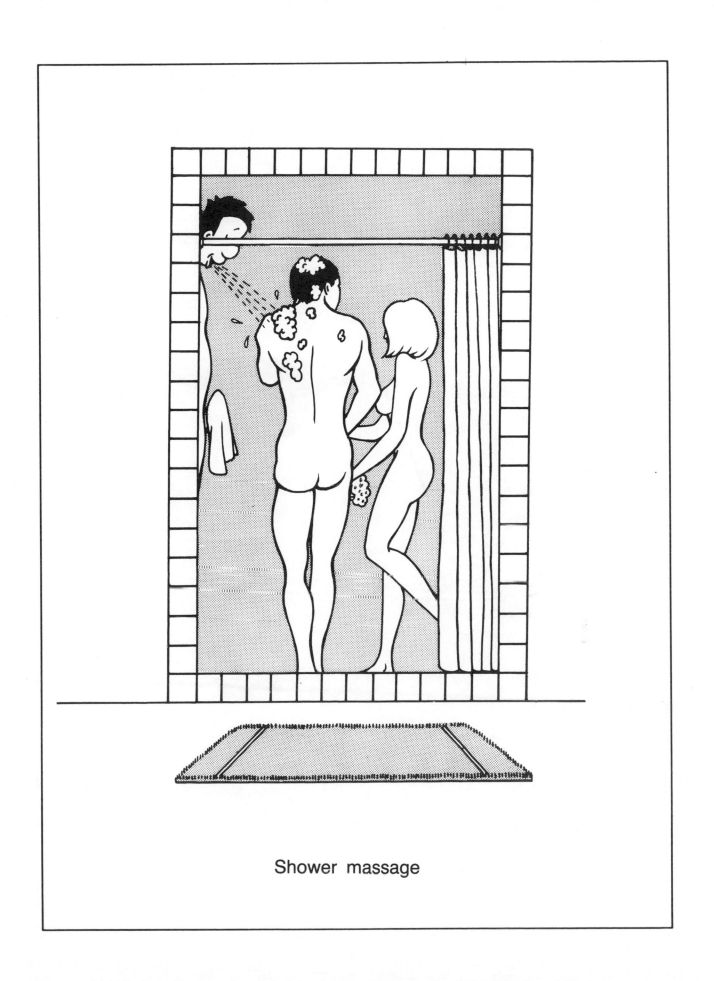

Shower massage

Enjoy his company on fishing trips

Entertain your girl friends

"Club Bed" memories

Dogs best friend

Window display for the holidays

Volunteer him for nativity work

The swinger

Pin the tail on daddy

Piñata

Lounge chair for the pool

HOT! Cool off with a beer

CHAPTER
THREE

HOW TO USE A DEAD
HUSBAND FOR...
FULFILLING YOUR NEEDS

Perfect listener

Take out your frustrations

Sample different hair styles without ruining your own

Hog all the covers, without complaints

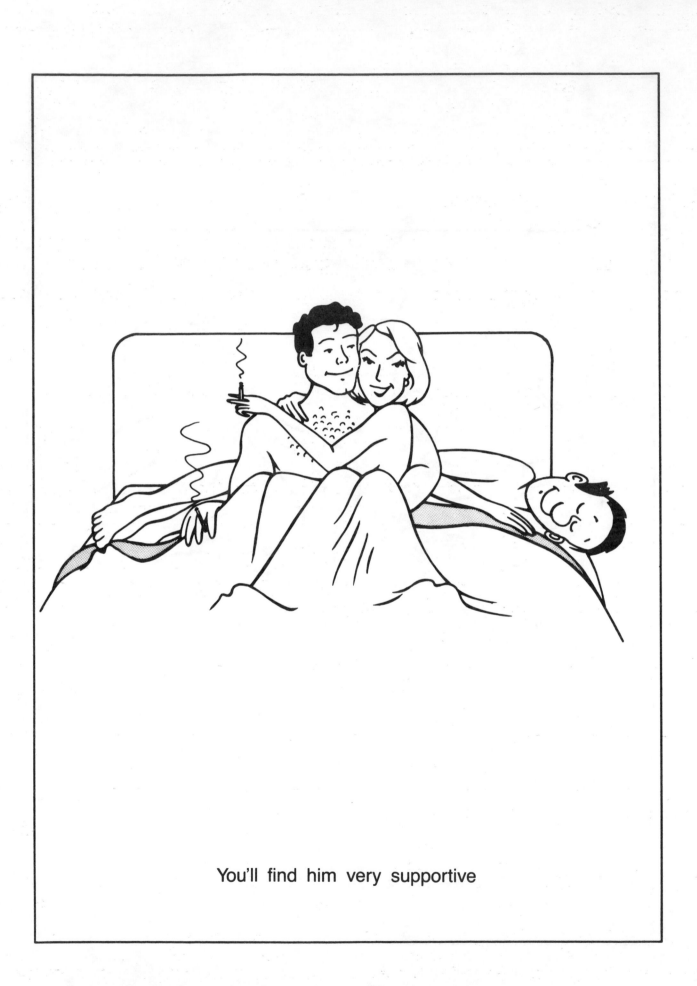

You'll find him very supportive

Weight loss incentive

Charge tons of clothing with his credit cards. . .
and enjoy his big smile

The stiff

Feel secure your toilet seat will always be down and dry...

Dead weight

Never bar-hop alone

Sample men in different uniforms without being promiscuous

Take him to science class

Show off your popularity by every so often
placing him at the front door

The closet's all yours - his wardrobe is on his back

CHAPTER
FOUR

HOW TO USE A DEAD
HUSBAND FOR...
**EARNING EXTRA INCOME
AND CUTTING EXPENSES**

Lease him to a Hollywood studio for stunt work

Earn extra dollars for your new mink

Earn extra income

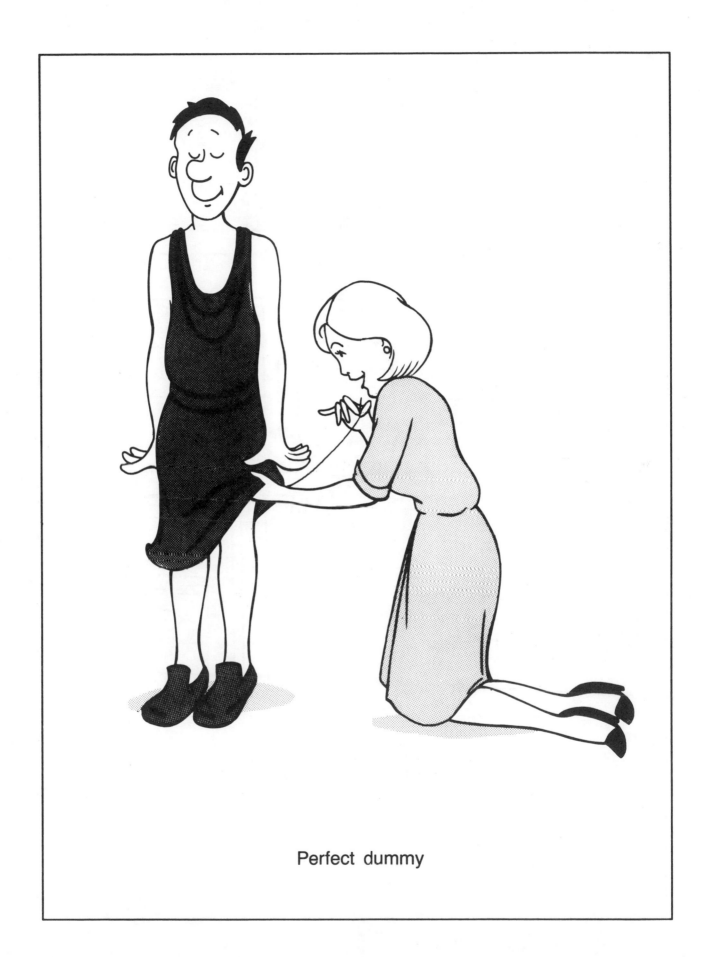

Perfect dummy

Night watchman

Display advertising

Strip club signage

Do away with unwanted tickets

Lower your repair bills from unscrupulous mechanics

Soft cloth car wash

Lend him out for government service

Save on airfare

CHAPTER
FIVE

HOW TO USE A DEAD
HUSBAND FOR...
RECREATION

Scratching post

Make beautiful music together

Ride'm cowboy

Veg-A-Matic fisherman - the automatic fishing aid

Hard to find a Dad who enjoys sports with the kids

Bone for the dog

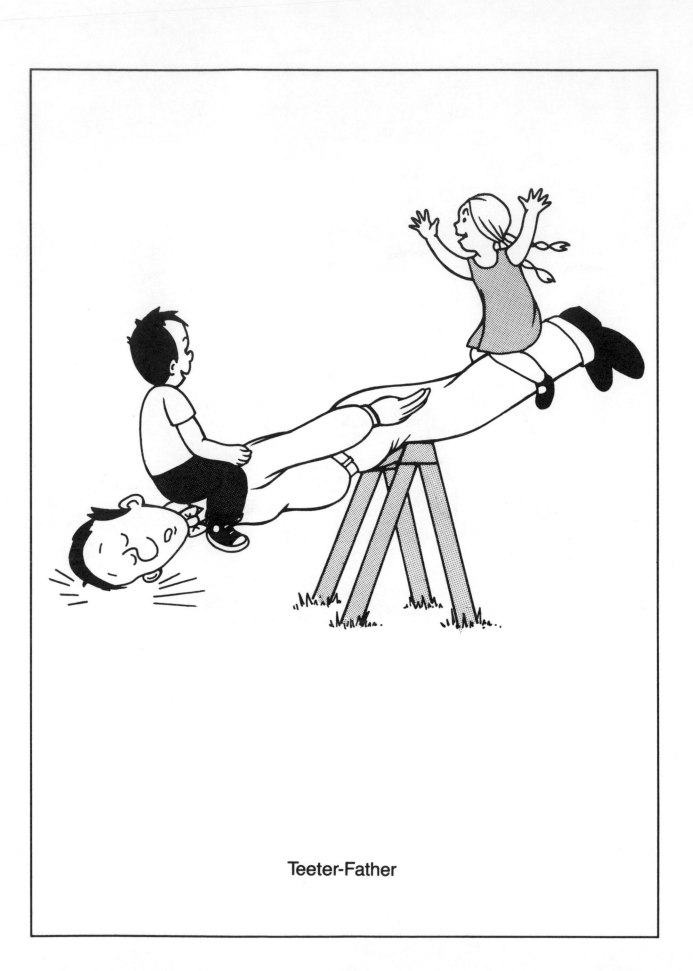

Teeter-Father

Dead ringer

Jumping *JACK*

Stiff platform

Protect *his* boat

Keep cool

Test pilot

CHAPTER
SIX

HOW TO USE A DEAD
HUSBAND FOR...
EMERGENCY SITUATIONS

Jack-ASS

Place him in front of window. . .
while you are away on trips

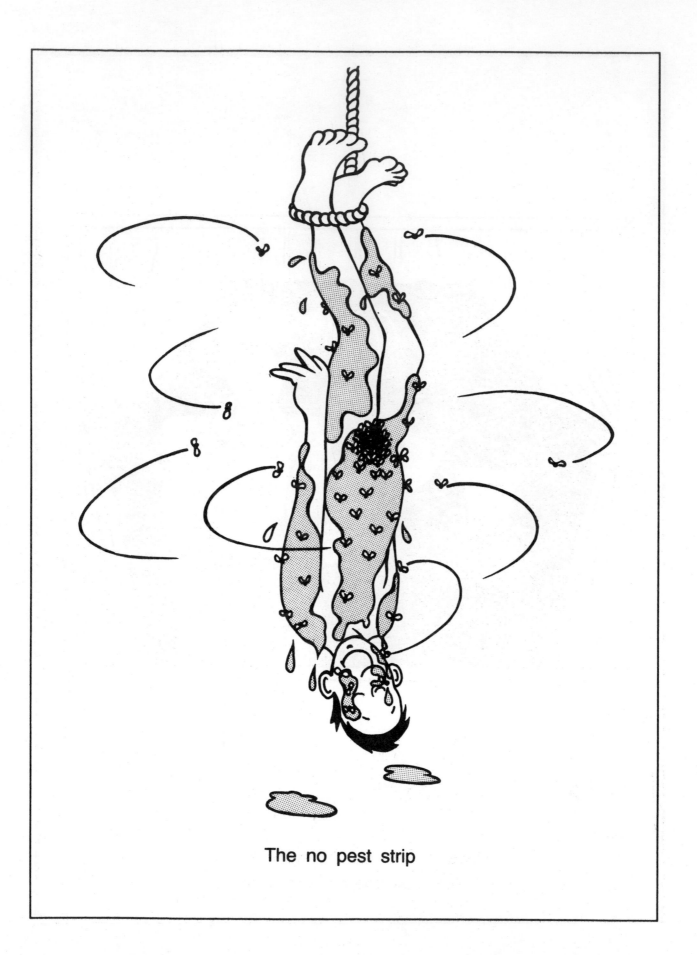

The no pest strip

Officer, I was speeding to the hospital he just...

When the conversation dies

Let the Harai Krishna's have someone to talk to when they visit

Protect your garden

Stamp licker

Mother-in-law deterrent

Mr. Plunger

Camouflage the mousetrap

Turn off your nerdy dates

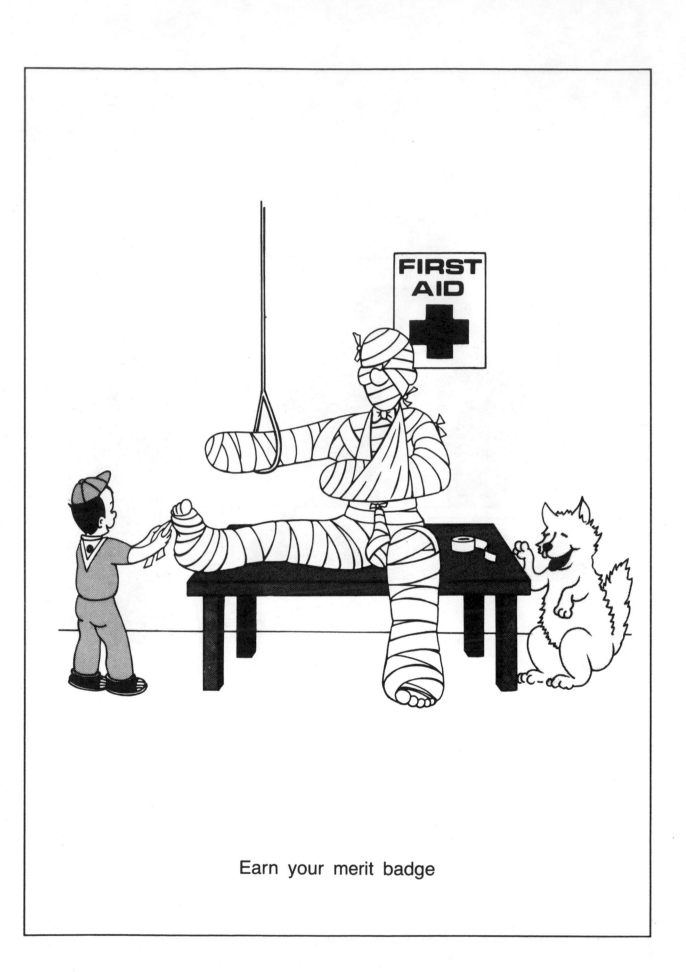

Earn your merit badge

Take him out on Father's Day so the kids
will know they have a father

Bankable, for a change

Discourage maids with sticky fingers

Clean-up fall leaves

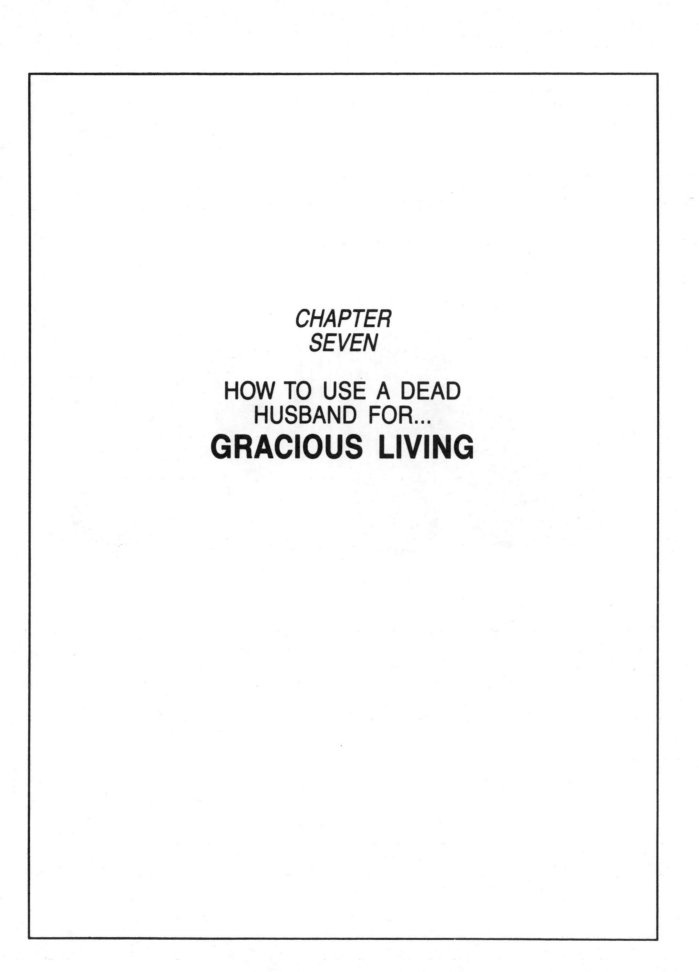

*CHAPTER
SEVEN*

HOW TO USE A DEAD
HUSBAND FOR...
GRACIOUS LIVING

Book ends

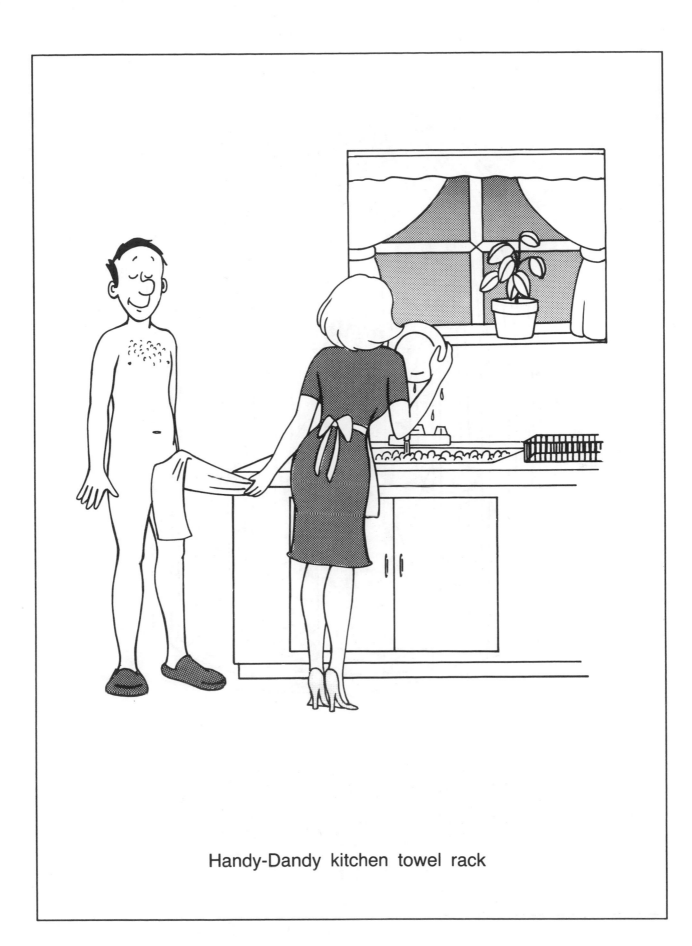

Handy-Dandy kitchen towel rack

Classic bird stand

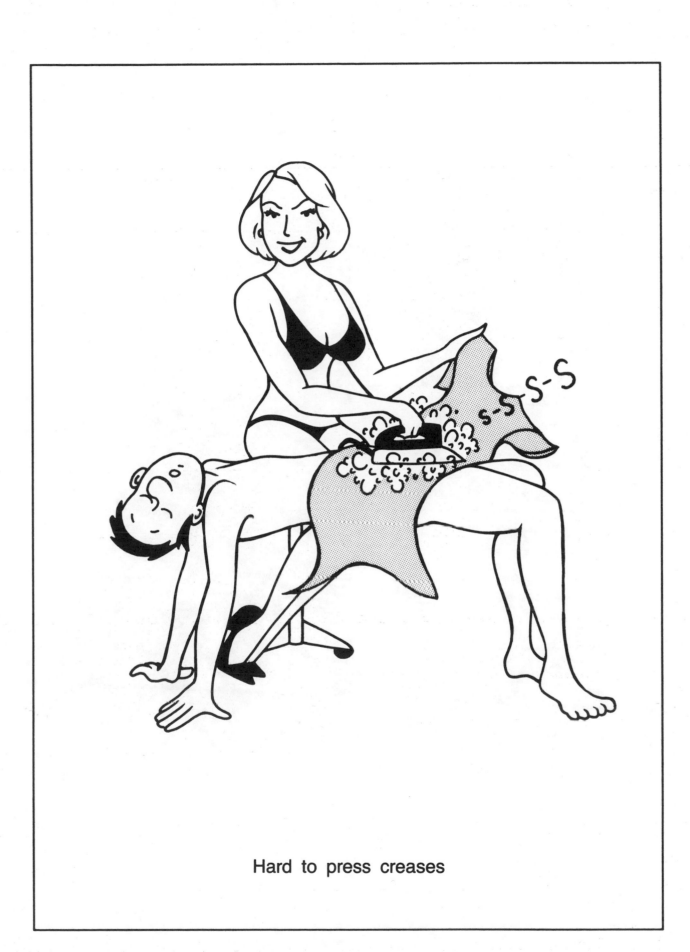

Hard to press creases

Night light

Flexible mop

Improve T.V. reception

Happy holidays

Playing our song

Doorman

Mr. Greenjeans

Gives good phone

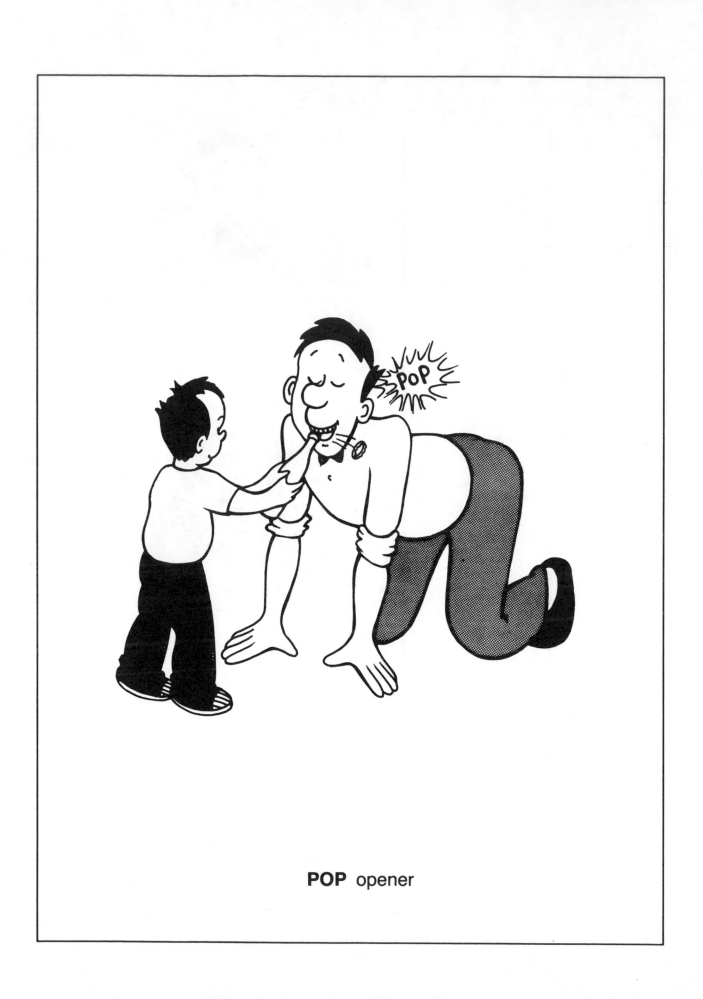

POP opener

CHAPTER
EIGHT

HOW TO USE A DEAD
HUSBAND FOR...
GETTING AROUND TOWN

Roll-A-Dad

Take him on a second honeymoon

Hood ornament

Take him shopping with you

Adjustable bike rack

Traction in winter

Get to work faster

Childs safety seat

Hope you enjoyed that feeling of Total Power.
Let's now return to reality.
Where we strive for a perfect imbalance
between men and women.

———